I0554773

JESUS

The Path to Victorious Living

I can do all things through **CHRIST**

which strengthened me.

(Philippians 4:13)

Dr. Annette M. West

JESUS

The Path to Victorious Living

Copyright©2004 by Annette West

Revised 2022

Printed in the United States of America

ISBN: 9781980350583
Library of Congress Control Number: 2022907391

by *JANE* Publishing

Spiritual -- Christian -- Daily Living -- Bible Study
Teaching Source --Empowerment

Acknowledgments

First, I acknowledge Jesus Christ as my personal Lord and Savior. Never can I say enough about how wonderful You are in my life. You have done so much for me and brought me a mighty long way to this appointed time, and I say thank You.

My most profound appreciation to my husband, John; you love me unconditionally. You are my rock. Thank you for supporting the work that God has set before me. You are a gift to my life, and I love and treasure you.

To my children, Terrence, Nikki, and Ebonee, I love you, and thank you for showing your love to me and sharing your life experiences.

To my ministry sisters, Annette Alvizures and Yolanda Whitehead, for answering my call for assistance in editing my work. It is a pleasure to work with you, and I honor our time together.

Thank you to the many people I have encountered within and outside the church who encouraged me to move forward in God's calling upon my life. Thus, a special thank you to Bishop Leepolian and Prophetess Virginia Turner for modeling the love of the Lord with integrity and challenging me in my early years of ministry in Germany.

Finally, to my Mother Marie and Auntie Linda, you are beautiful to me. Our conversations are always enlightening. I love you and pray for your continued longevity of life!

Table of Contents

Introduction 7

Chapter One: Victorious 13

Chapter Two: Believe it 25

Chapter Three: Testing and Trials 35

Chapter Four: Praying Through It 45

Chapter Five: HIS Promises 53

Chapter Six: Perseverance 63

Chapter Seven: Focus on Him 71

Chapter Eight: Peace 81

Final Thoughts 91

Prayer for a Victorious Life 95

Scripture List 99

The Lord's Prayer 101

The Visionary: Dr. Annette West 102

Other Books by Dr. Annette West 104

Upcoming Author Projects 105

Write – Writer – Writing 106

Introduction

In this life, you are not alone on this journey. Every person goes through seasons of difficulty and challenges. This book aims to share with you that no matter what is going on in your life. Victory is available.

> Many are the afflictions of the righteous, but the LORD delivers him out of them all. (Psalm 34:19)

The enemy, Satan, has many tactics and traps that he will use to get a person off track. He will isolate and convince you that you won't make it. He will work hard to make you think you are a failure and will not succeed.

The good news is that God promises He will deliver the righteous ones out of all afflictions. When a person accepts Christ as their personal Lord and Savior, an intimate relationship begins with Him. Faith in Him makes this relationship available.

If you are going through a tough time today, keep an attitude of faith and expectancy. Declare His promises over your life. You are more than a conqueror through Him, as the joy of the Lord is your strength! Victory is before you as you continue to stand, even during difficult times. It might be today, next week, next month, or even next year; hold on, for God is faithful and true to His Word! Through faith and patience, you will inherit the promise, it may take time, but it will come. Stay on this journey; you shall find victory to have the abundant life that God desires for you.

God is the one Who can give us the victory through whatever is going on in our lives. Although you have days that seem more overcast and bleaker than others, you will make it through.

Be assured that God has a plan and purpose for your life. A significant part of His purpose is to be VICTORIOUS in your daily walk. So, when it seems that you have struggled long and hard against your opponent, the adversary, know that VICTORY will come. God needs you to stay focused, trust, and believe in the plan for your life.

But thanks be to God, which giveth us the victory through our Lord Jesus Christ.
(1 Corinthians 15:57)

You will triumph over the enemy. Jesus already paid the price for your freedom. Now, walk into what God has already planned for your life.

Believe that God created the heavens and the earth and that you exist because He loves you and wants you here. God will reward those who research Him and believe God can do exceedingly abundantly above everything you can ever ask or think about today.

God desires His children to walk victoriously in every area of their life. Including your family, finances, health, etc. You are God's prized possession, created in His image, and God wants only the best for you. Thus, you believe that in Christ Jesus, you are more than a conqueror.

And we know that all things work together for good to them that love God, to them who are the called according to His purpose. (Romans 8:28)

Within the pages of this book, the hope is to take you on a journey, sharing a few fundamental principles I believe can bring you VICTORY as you walk with God. You will gain a clear understanding of applying basic principles in this book to your daily walk. My prayer is that you are enriched as you walk with Him, and your eyes are opened.

We will review scriptures, share thoughts, answer questions, journal, and pray. You can check all scriptures in your study time. Also, if you choose to use a different version of the Bible, align it with the KJV used throughout this book.

Victorious Living!

Chapter One

But thanks be to God,
which gives us the victory through
our Lord Jesus Christ.

(1 Corinthians 15:57)

VICTORIOUS

To have victory over sin, you must have a life in Christ. You need to know that Christ came to give you abundant life in Him. Make this personal; walk and live in Him without a defeated mentality, which happens as your mind is transformed. The things of the world quickly crowd our thinking and make it harder for our minds to be changed, but it can happen. The Bible says,

> I beseech you, therefore, brethren, by the mercies of God, that ye present your bodies a living sacrifice, holy, acceptable unto God, which is your reasonable service.

And be not conformed to this world: but be ye transformed by the renewing of your mind, that ye may prove what is that good, and acceptable, and perfect, will of God.

(Romans 12:1-2)

If a person's mind is stuck in the past, the negative, the things of the world, it will be impossible to see the newness of life. Having a renewed mind allows one to look at life differently, with a clear view.

Some people know that victory is possible because they have seen it happen for others; it, however, does not seem to come to them. They genuinely love the Lord but can't shake the thorn that appears to keep them with a defeated mindset. They seem to forget that none is perfect and that there is something in every person's life that has haunted them before and possibly still does.

Everyone has a past, but if God threw it in the sea of forgetfulness, why not leave it there. Anything, from something as simple as lying or gossiping to things like pornography, homosexuality, lust, bitterness, pride, alcohol, drug addiction, gossiper or busybody, and many other things.

> But if ye be led of the Spirit, ye are not under the law. Now the works of the flesh are manifest, which are these; Adultery, fornication, uncleanness, lasciviousness, Idolatry, witchcraft, hatred, variance, emulations, wrath, strife, seditions, heresies, envying's, murders, drunkenness, reveling, and such like: of the which I tell you before, as I have also told you in time past, that they which do such things shall not inherit the kingdom of God. (Galatians 5:18-21)

Yet, the Bible declares that sin shall not have dominion over us, nor should we be servants of sin. So why do so many Christians continue to live in bondage to sin?

Even Paul, the apostle, remarked concerning his early experience as a Christian,

> For I know that in me (that is, in my flesh) dwells no good thing: to will is present with me; but how to perform that which is good I find not. For the good that I would I do not: but the evil, which I would not, that I do. For I delight in the law of God after the inward man: but I see another law in my members, warring against the law of my mind, and bringing me into captivity to the law of sin, which is in my members. O wretched man that I am! who shall deliver me from the body of this death?" (Romans 7:18-19, 22-24)

According to Paul, Christians today want to do better but cannot. They do the very thing they desire not to do. Their flesh is weak. They seem not to understand how to perform that which is good. They delight in God's law and wish to serve the Lord in holiness, but there is a war inside them, bringing them into captivity to the law of sin. Paul's statement echoes the words of many Christians living in despair.

> O wretched man that I am! who shall deliver
> me from this body of death?
> (Romans 7:24)

Christians often feel like they are fighting for their lives in the battle against sin and losing, believing they no longer have control of the situation. They have become a servant to sin. Thus, the Christian has no joy and lives in fear because of this intense battle. They are afraid to step out and fight for fear of failing again. Like Saul and the armies of Israel, they feel that they cannot be victorious. They feel

> dismayed and greatly afraid.
> (1 Samuel 17:11)

To continually be victorious, Christians must learn to stand firm and not fail in their struggle against sin. They may attempt to fight against sin, the enemy, using man's methods, as in the story of David and Goliath. Saul's armor was man's method. So, David took off Saul's armor and went out to face Goliath armed with only a staff, his sling, and five smooth stones. David boasted to Goliath, this giant of a man,

> Thou comest to me with a sword and with a spear and with a shield. But I come to thee in the name of the Lord of hosts.
> (1 Samuel 17:45)

Saul's armor would never work for David, and the armor Goliath had would not work for him either. David continued,

> The Lord saves not with sword and spear, for the battle is the Lord's.
> (1 Samuel 17:47)

When you fight for your life, you will do whatever is necessary to be successful. If we think about David taking his sword and cutting off the head of Goliath, it does not paint a pretty picture. But it is something that we need to think about it. What are you going to do when the battle comes? How will you be able to stand amid the fight? It might not be your first choice, you might not like it, but it's what's necessary for victory.

Think about your being in a battle for your life against sin. Your KEY to VICTORY is to stand against and over the adversary. You can only win the battle with the proper armor. David was clothed only in the Spirit of the Lord. David focused on He who has ALL power. You need to know the battle is the Lord's; He will deliver the enemy into your hands! We must STOP! Put down the weapons we are trying to use and trust the Lord to have HIS proper armor for success.

Trust in the Lord with all thine heart; and lean not unto thine own understanding. In all thy ways acknowledge Him, and He shall direct thy paths.
(Proverbs 3:5-6)

Paul told the church in Ephesus that they could be strong. They needed to be prepared and equipped to stand during life issues.

Finally, my brethren, be strong in the Lord and the power of His might. Put on the whole armor of God, that ye may be able to stand against the devil's wiles. For we wrestle not against flesh and blood, but principalities, against powers, against the rulers of the darkness of this world, against spiritual wickedness in high places.
Wherefore take unto you the whole armor of God that ye may be able to withstand in the evil day, and having done all, to stand. Stand therefore, having your loins girt about with

truth, and having on the breastplate of righteousness; And your feet shod with the preparation of the gospel of peace; above all, taking the shield of faith, wherewith ye shall be able to quench all the fiery darts of the wicked. And take the helmet of salvation, and the sword of the Spirit, which is the Word of God.

(Ephesians 6:10-17)

When you are prepared for battle, can you "resist the devil, and he will flee from you." You have VICTORY! You can stand firm and go forth to battle with the faith of David, and the powers of the darkness of this world shall not stand against you.

Say this prayer before you continue to the next chapter!

Today Lord, I desire to begin a victorious journey with you. Open my eyes that I may see what your Word is saying to me for direction, in Jesus' name, Amen! Help me to stay focused through this book and on this journey.

Journal your thoughts from this chapter here!

_____

_____

_____

_____

_____

_____

_____

_____

_____

_____

_____

Chapter Two

I can do all things through Christ,

which strengthens me.

(Philippians 4:13)

BELIEVE

What you believe determines what you will do, act, and say. Thus, your belief is generated by faith in what you perceive as accurate. There are two elements to this belief:

(1) being convinced of the truth

(2) seizing the truth

God is what you need to believe in; however, Satan has always been and is still in the business of trying to deceive and lead people away from the Father. Satan deceives through the mind, bringing negative thoughts, telling you that you will not make it, and prompting you to behave unbecomingly to you and the Lord. He wants to make you think that everything you desire to do and or be is impossible. However, you need to shift your thinking and believe that in Christ Jesus, in Him, all things are possible. (Matthew 19:26)

It does not matter the situation; God can do the impossible. He is the Greatest One, able to do everything except fail.

God is the "I AM that I AM." (Exodus 3:14)

He is the one that is all that you need, even in the wilderness. (Joshua 5:5) He was everything the children of Israel needed, and He sustained them. Yet, sometimes people may say they believe this, but they act as if they are defeated. God expects us to have abundant, not mediocre, lives. So, believe that God can do everything but fail. We must take God at His Word and seek to live a life full of the abundance of His blessings.

We must believe the Word of God, trust in it, rely upon it, and act upon it constantly. One of my favorite scriptures is

> Trust in the Lord (the Word) with all thine heart and lean not unto thine own understanding. In all thy ways acknowledge Him (the Word), and He shall direct thy paths. (Proverbs 3:5-6)

We are easily deceived if we are not in tune with God's Word. The deception can often come through various avenues. However, anything that does not line up with the Word of God is a lie, and you should not listen to it. The Word of God says,

> Let God be true, but let every man be a liar (Romans 3:4)

Satan can easily seduce the mind when we are not in the right relationship with the Lord. Then again, it is his job to do everything he can to get your mind on anything other than godly things. We must never forget that the Word of God has not changed, and there is nothing new under the sun; it may just be packaged differently.

> Jesus Christ is the same yesterday, and today and forever. (Hebrews 13:8)

Satan went to Jesus after fasting for 40 days and 40 nights and trying to tempt Him away from God. He informed Jesus he had power, that if Jesus would bow down, he could receive. The great thing is that Jesus is the Word, and He knew the Word to remind Satan of what the Word said.

> Then was Jesus led up the Spirit into the wilderness to be tempted by the devil. And when he had fasted forty days and forty nights, he afterward hungered. And when the tempter came to him, he said, if thou be the Son of God, command that these stones be made bread. But he answered and said, It is written,

Man shall not live by bread alone, but by every Word that proceedeth out of the mouth of God. Then the devil taketh him up into the holy city, and setteth him on a pinnacle of the temple, And saith unto him, If thou be the Son of God, cast thyself down: for it is written, He shall give his angels charge concerning thee: and in [their] hands they shall bear thee up, lest at any time thou dash thy foot against a stone.

Jesus said unto him, It is written again, Thou shalt not tempt the Lord thy God. Furthermore, the devil taketh Him up into an exceeding high mountain, and sheweth Him all the kingdoms of the world, and the glory of them; And saith unto him, All these things will I give thee, if thou wilt fall and worship me Then saith Jesus unto him, Get thee hence, Satan: for it is written, Thou shalt worship the Lord thy God, and Him only shalt thou serve. Then the devil leaveth Him, and behold, angels came and ministered unto Him. (Matthew 4:1-11)

We must work to have faith to please God, a belief that develops and grows as we spend more time daily in God's presence. The more we hear the Word and learn to apply it to our lives, the better prepared we are when Satan is on his job and trying to create havoc in our lives. Thus, we must learn what God's Word declares so that we will be full of His Truth. The following scriptures are a few ways to help you focus on God's Word.

So, then faith cometh by hearing and hearing by the Word of God. (Romans 10:17)

Study to show thyself approved unto God a workman that needeth not to be ashamed, rightly dividing the Word of truth. (Romans 10:17)

If ye abide in me and my words abide in you, ye shall ask what ye will, and it shall be done unto you.

(John 15:7)

Our strength comes as we are connected to the vine. However, deception can come from anyone; family, friends, loved ones, church pews, news media, government officials, doctors, lawyers, etc. Anything you come across that is contrary to the Word of God is a lie, and do not try to sugarcoat it. God always has scriptures to back up everything. Use two or three scriptures to make sure you confirm what God's Word is saying.

Say this prayer before you move to the next section:

Father in heaven, I desire to believe that you are the beginning and end of everything. I ask that You help me daily seek Your face and keep my faith in You and not allow Satan to deceive me with his many vices in this world; in Jesus' name, Amen!

Journal Your Thoughts from this Chapter Here!

_____

_____

_____

_____

_____

_____

_____

_____

_____

_____

_____

Chapter Three

Rejoicing in hope; patient in tribulation;

continuing instant in prayer;

(Romans 12:12)

Testing Will Come

No one is immune from sin. Every person has been enticed, at some point, to act in ways unbecoming to the Lord. We are tested, temptation all around. Jesus said to his disciples:

> Things that cause people to sin are bound to come, but woe to that person through whom they come. (Luke 17:1)

The enticement is to do something you know you should not but still do it. Paul shares his inability to do what he should when he knew it and did not understand his behavior.

For that which I do I allow not: for what I would, that do I not; but what I hate, that do I. If then I do that which I would not, I consent unto the law that [it is] good. Now then, it is no more I that do it, but sin that dwelleth in me, for I know that in me (that is, in my flesh,) dwelleth no good thing: for to will is present with me; but [how] to perform that which is good I find not. For the good that I would I do not: but the evil I would not, that I do. Now, if I do that, I would not; it is no more I that do it, but sin that dwelleth in me. (Roman 7:15-20)

Testing is what we must go through to learn a lesson. People think they shouldn't go through anything wrong and that bad things don't happen to Christians. If you don't go through anything, how do you know you have the stamina to endure and develop the right relationship with God? I always say that without a test, there can be no testimony. This testing generates a testimony for you to tell people how good/great God is and how He brought you through. Just know that if He did it for you once, He could do it again.

> Blessed [is] the man that endureth temptation: for when he is tried, he shall receive the crown of life, which the Lord hath promised to them that love him. Let no man say when he is tempted, I am tempted of God: for God cannot be tempted with evil, neither tempteth any man: But every man is tempted, when he is drawn away of his lust, and enticed. Then when lust hath conceived, it bringeth forth sin: and sin, when it is finished, bringeth forth death. (James 1: 12-15)

Trials come to us to see if we are strong enough to stand firm in our connection to the Lord. Satan attacked everything Job had. He, Satan, believed that Job would be tempted to curse God, but Job refused to allow his downtrodden situation to speak a negative word against His God.

> Now there was a day when the sons of God came to present themselves before the LORD, and Satan came also among them.
> (Job 1:6)

Think about this; God created you; He knows your daily walk. He knows those who are strong in Him, so sometimes He allows the negative situations to come our way. Satan sees your daily walk, and sometimes God will let Satan put some unimaginable conditions in your way. He may allow Satan to attack your health, family, and finances.

The devil tempted Jesus. After He had fasted for forty days and forty nights, the devil came to Him in His weak state. The great thing was that Jesus knew the Father. When you know the Father, think about this: you have something to stand on, something to fight with, the Word.

We will address this further here. There are three things that Jesus knew about his strength while being tested. Found in Matthew 4.

1. Jesus knew that He could do without the physical bread if He had the Father. (4:4) Your body can go without food for a reasonable time. Most doctors agree that a healthy person can go up to eight weeks without food if they have water.

2. Jesus told the devil don't try to put God to the test. (4:7) Since God initially created all things, one would be a fool to think they can offer you what already belongs to God.

3. Jesus told the devil that He could only worship the Father. (4:10) Just as we are created in God's image, to worship Him and send up sweet smell to his nostrils.

Through it all, Jesus clarifies that there is one thing the devil can't touch, and that is His relationship with God. We should be able to say the same thing. Satan does what he will, but we will not curse the God we serve.

We can learn much from the examples of Jesus and Job when temptation came their way.

1. Know Who God is.
2. Know the Word of God

Each person must have a firm foundation to stand on, to be strengthened by the situation. We know the devil does not have ultimate power when God is involved in our lives.

God, at some point, will call you to work and empower you. With full assurance, as you seek to please God, be assured that Satan will be there working to get you off-track, tempting you.

And Jesus, when he was baptized, went up straightway out of the water: and, lo, the heavens were opened unto him, and he saw the Spirit of God descending like a dove, and lighting upon him: And lo a voice from heaven, saying, This is my beloved Son, in whom I am well pleased. (Matthew 3:16-17)

We need to recognize that this testing benefits our Christian growth walk. When you are tested and overcome, your testimony shares the depth of God's grace and how He sustained you during your testing. You shall be empowered to sustain whatever comes your way. Jesus went into this testing only after the Father had empowered him in the Spirit.

We will not go through anything new. Thus, we must know that anything that happens to us has happened to someone else before us. (Ecclesiastes 1:9) We can stand and bear it when we are in Christ Jesus and that God has already made a way of escape. The situation may not be over quickly, but it means that God will be with you no matter what you are going through. In Christ Jesus, we can pass every test and temptation that the devil sends our way.

We can be empowered and stand firm in the test, the mess, whatever it is—constantly reminding ourselves that God is Bigger and Wiser and more Powerful than anything we encounter in this world and can see us through.

Say this prayer before moving to the next chapter:

I am enriched today, Father. I recognize that others have endured and set the example for my success as I am going through. Jesus, help me remain strong during testing. Thank you for the tests that have come my way. I am stronger and have a testimony to share with others to encourage them. Amen!

Journal Your Thoughts from this Chapter Here!

_____

_____

_____

_____

_____

_____

_____

_____

_____

_____

_____

Chapter Four

Pray without ceasing

(I Thessalonians 5:17)

PRAYING Through It

Prayer is essential for our daily existence. Issues will arise, and we must pray until we receive the peace in our spirit that it has been done. We must pray in all situations, but first, we need to learn how to pray.

Where can we find our prayer example? There are several passages of scripture to assist in this effort. Take time to review the below scriptures. Write what each is saying to you concerning prayer for your life in a few words. Think about how each scripture will help you move forward in your prayer life, and write a thought from each.

Matthew 6: 5-16

_____

_____

_____

I Thessalonians 5:17

_____

_____

_____

Ephesians 6:18

_____

_____

_____

Philippians 4:6

_____

_____

_____

We cannot survive in our relationship with God without prayer. We need to be mindful that our relationship with God is personal, not public, as prayer is not a spectator sport but a heart-felt offering of petitions before the throne. Our acts of prayer are of devotion and should be in a secret place. (Matthew 6:5-8) This is important because we aren't trying to win a reputation for eloquent speaking before others but intimacy with our Lord.

Our prayers should be personal and express our delight in God's will and dependence on Him. (Matthew 6: 9-13) The foundation of prayer is a personal relationship with God as your Father. We should relate to God in the model prayer with the following thoughts.

- Recognition of Him as "in heaven" and "hallowed" (set apart and holy) puts us in the proper frame of mind as we come to Him. We are reminded that we are holy because of Who He is.

- "Your kingdom come" is an expression of our

willingness to surrender to His will now, that He might rule in our lives.

- We trust God so much that we ask only for Him to meet our everyday needs. The request for "daily bread" – which does
not mean wealth – expresses both dependences on Him and confidence in Him.

- "Forgive us" expresses our awareness that we fall short in all things and rely on a constant flow of God's grace.

- For if ye forgive men their trespasses, your heavenly Father will also forgive you: But if ye forgive not men their trespasses, neither will your Father, forgive your trespasses. (Matthew 6:14-15)

Don't worry if you don't know what to pray. God has all the answers. He knows what you don't know and will intercede for you. Trust him that you believe He will come through for you with your heart.

Although I share this with you, there is no formula for prayer. However, Jesus left this example that we can use when we don't know what to pray; The Lord's Prayer. Yet, we must not allow The Lord's Prayer to become a repetitive effort without a revelation of Him. We must submit ourselves before the throne with a heart of gratitude in awe of His greatness. Our attitude makes the difference when we pray in our approach to God our Father through His Son Jesus.

Here are some ways in which we can pray:

- PRAY before you rise in the morning. Recognize that God has allowed you to live another day.
- PRAY when you don't know what to do. God has all the answers, so seek Him for direction.
- PRAY when you think you know what to do. God will guide you to ensure you use your will correctly for His benefit.

- PRAY when you don't know what to say. God will give you the correct answer.
- PRAY always. When you feel like it and when you don't.

You know that the enemy, with his rebellious spirits, does not want you to spend time in prayer. He knows that when you do, you will be strengthened. So, when you pray, always say, "Thy will be done." Critically important since we do not know God's direction for our life all the time. Remember, it's about what He wants for your life and not our selfish desires. We must learn how to ask God to show us His desires for our lives as His purpose and goals are revealed.

Say this prayer before you move to the next chapter:

Thank you, Father, for the example you have left me to learn how to pray in such a way that pleases you. I desire to come before you daily in a secret place to pray before your throne. Help me be committed to this and not be concerned with eloquent words, but a relationship commitment to you, in Jesus' name, Amen!

Journal Your Thoughts from this Chapter Here!

_____

_____

_____

_____

_____

_____

_____

_____

_____

Chapter Five

Don't let the book of the law
depart from your mouth, meditate on it
day and night then you will be careful to
do everything written in it.

(Joshua 1:8)

HIS PROMISES

In the many years of my activity in ministry, I have come across too many people that think that because they accepted Jesus Christ as their Lord and Savior, there is nothing else they need to do. They forget that faith without works is dead. It is not just being saved but living a daily life committed to following Christ's principles. We must purpose in our hearts to work and ensure our life measures up to the examples found in Christ's legacy.

Even so faith, if it hath not works, is dead, being alone. (James 2:17)

There are times when people come to the Father through the Son with requests and petitions and think it will be done. Sometimes those requests are out of order.

> Ye ask, and receive not, because ye ask amiss, that ye may consume it upon your lusts. (James 4:3)

Just because we are saved does not mean that God will do everything we ask of Him, especially if we ask amiss, and it is not in His will. However, there are some things that He will do if we do our part.

A promise is an assurance that one will or will not do something. The promise provides a basis for expecting something from someone. Many promises within the Bible are for us if we follow biblical principles.

In the Bible, we can find God's promises to His people. However, many of those promises have conditions attached. There's a stipulation with the promise. You must do something, put forth some effort, for it to come to pass. Some examples of promises with conditions:

In the opening of the Old Testament "O.T." book of Joshua, we find God preparing Joshua for his role as the new leader of the people of Israel. He was destined to be the spiritual and military leader of God's people during the conquest of Canaan, the Promised Land.

1. **Promise** -- I will give you every place where you set your foot, as I promised Moses.

> *Condition* -- get ready to cross the Jordan River into the land I am about to give to them—to the Israelites. (Joshua 1:1-2)
>
> *The effort* to push forth for the promise and condition – Preparation is needed to receive what God promises.

2. **Promise**- you will lead these people to inherit the land I swore to their ancestors to give them.

> *Condition* -- Be strong and courageous. (Joshua 1:8)

The effort of the promise and condition – You must be firm with the tenacity to lead and receive what God has for you.

3. **Promise** – You will be prosperous and successful.

   Condition – Don't let the book of the law depart from your mouth, meditate on it day and night, and you will be careful to do everything written in it. (Joshua 1:8)

   The effort of the promise and condition – Stay committed and follow God's teachings day and night to succeed in your life.

4. **Promise** – The Lord, your God, will be with you wherever you go.

   Condition – Be strong and courageous, do not be terrified. (Joshua 1:9)

   The effort of the promise and condition – No fear but strength is needed for God is with you always.

The O.T. book of Proverbs is a collection of advice and counsel intended to guide the reader's practical and moral choices. An individual who truly fears God by holding Him in awe will make prudent (right) choices and can expect to live a secure and happy life. A few promises and conditions are below:

1. **Promise** – prolong the life of many years and bring you peace and prosperity.

> *Condition* – Do not forget my teaching but keep my commandments in your heart. (Proverbs 3:1)
>
> *The effort* of the promise and condition – Keep God's commandments so you may have a long life.

2. **Promise** – He will direct your path.

> *Condition* – Trust in the Lord with all heart and mind and lean not on your understanding, in all thy ways, acknowledge Him. (Proverbs 3:5-6)

The effort of the promise and condition – Trust God with your whole being, and He will direct you through life.

Minimal thought was shared on O.T. promises and conditions in the previous pages. We will look at a few promises and conditions from the New Testament (N.T.).

1. **Promise** – All things will be added unto you.

   Condition – Seek you first the kingdom of God and His righteousness (Matthew 6:33)

   The effort of the promise and condition – Seek God and His kingdom before all else, and He will add what is needed to your life.

2.   **Promise** - You will be saved.

   Condition - Confess with thy mouth and believe in thy heart that God raised Jesus from the dead. (Romans 10: 9-10)

   The effort of the promise and condition – Say with your mouth and spirit move within you that Jesus is God's Son and died and now lives so you can be saved.

3. **Promise** – Resist the devil, and he will flee from you.

Condition – Submit yourselves, then to God.

(James 4:7)

The effort of the promise and condition – Must submit to God, and then you are strong enough to tell the devil to move from your presence.

God has some great promises for us in His Word. It does not matter how powerful Satan is, with his support team working to keep you from meeting the conditions. God is more and most powerful. Thus, Satan will not be able to prevail in our lives, and we can flee from him. However, this is only possible when we submit ourselves to God. Our God has so much planned for us. He desires prosperity for our success, but we must align ourselves with His Word.

_____

Say this prayer before you move to the next chapter:

Father, thank You for the many promises that You for me in Your Word. To receive the promise, I must align with Your Word. Help me stay focused on Your Word and strive to do that written in Your Word, in Jesus' name, Amen.

Journal Your Thoughts from this Chapter Here!

_____

_____

_____

_____

_____

_____

_____

_____

_____

_____

_____

_____

Chapter Six

Knowing this, that the trying of your faith
worketh patience.
(James 1:3)

PERSEVERANCE

———————

Persistence is when one is insistent on seeking what they want and will request it until it is received. The persistent person must be willing to hold firmly and steadfastly to a purpose, despite the obstacles, warnings, or setbacks. They are repetitive or tenacious (firm) until the expectation is received.

Have you ever wanted something so bad that you would not let it up until you received it? Sometimes, you drove the other person crazy, so they eventually gave in to you. You had a determination and would not let go until your desires had been met. It reminds me of Jacob wrestling through the night with God and saying he would not let go until he was blessed.

> And Jacob was left alone, and there wrestled a man with him until the breaking of the day. And when he saw that he prevailed not against him, he touched the hollow of his thigh; and the hollow of Jacob's thigh was out of joint, as he wrestled with him. And he said, Let me go, for the day breaketh. And he said, I will not let thee go, except thou bless me. (Genesis 32: 24-26)

Our relationship is to be with God. He already knows what you need, but he desires that you make your request known to Him. Don't give up; hold on to Him through the process to attain your needs. You can get it through man if God desires, not necessarily because they want to give it to you, but because you just won't go away. An excellent example of this is the woman that kept going to judge. He kept refusing her until she got on his nerves, and he gave her what she requested.

> And there was a widow in that city; and she came unto him, saying, Avenge me of my adversary. And he would not go for a while: but afterward, he said within himself, Though I fear not God, nor regard man; Yet because this widow troubleth me, I will avenge her, lest by her continual coming she weary me.
> (Luke 18:3-5)

We must learn to endure, continue in our request, last, and abide, never wavering. If you want it, you must be willing to ask for it. In the book of Luke, Jesus continues with His teaching to the disciples on how to pray. Two parables will be addressed here in hopes of giving a clearer perspective.

The ***first parable*** is of the ***friend needing bread***. Here Luke shares that one must be persistent if they want something and gives an example of one's friend in need and continuing to ask for provision until it is received. The friend needed bread to feed the children, even annoyed the person until they met their request. These are two great examples of persistence. Take some time before continuing to read the following passages. (Luke 11:5-13)

The ***second parable*** is of the ***persistent widow***. This parable teaches the necessity of patience, persistence, and persevering prayer. Though delivered in different situations, both parables show a person granting a request because of their selfish motives. The Persistent Friend's persevering prayer is for what is needed to sustain, and the Persistent Widow is for protection. (Luke 18:1-8)

Read both passages of scriptures, as they are both great reminders to us of the importance of staying firm in our request for the Lord to act and never lose hope. Don't let anyone tell you that you cannot attain it if you want it. It's up to you to put forth the effort and make your request known. We need to believe that what we want is available to us beyond adversity that may say otherwise. We should continue without halting until we have what we desire and need unless we hear God say NO.

Say this prayer before moving to the next chapter:

Father, I believe that You have everything I need to be successful. I must believe that You will come through as I remain strong and firm in my persistence as I come to You. Thank You for being the God that will meet my needs in Jesus' name.

Journal Your Thoughts from this Chapter Here!

_____

_____

_____

_____

_____

_____

_____

_____

_____

_____

_____

Chapter Seven

Let us fix our eyes on Jesus, the author and
finisher of our faith, who for the joy that was
set before Him endured the cross, scorning
its shame, and sat down at the right hand of
the throne of God.

(Hebrews 12:2)

FOCUS on Him

When I want to focus on something, I set my view, my eyes, on that thing. It is like when looking through a pair of binoculars. I sat at my front window and looked through binoculars to see the woodpecker up in the tree. I must take my time and focus on the lenses to see clearly at a distance. If my focus is off, I may be looking at the limb on a tree and miss the bird.

Think about it; we typically set our sights, focusing on things of interest. Watch then turn the lenses until the picture becomes clear. When the picture becomes clear, nothing is there to distort your view. However, the focus is distorted if we turn the lens.

We should put our focus on Jesus. Drawing closer to God is a primary way to maintain spiritual focus.

> Let us fix our eyes on Jesus, the author and perfector of our faith, who for the joy set before Him endured the cross, scorning its shame, and sat down at the right hand of the throne of God. (Hebrews 12:2)

> Draw near to God, and He will draw near to you. Cleanse your hands, you sinners; and purify your hearts, you double-minded. Be afflicted, and mourn, and weep: let your laughter be turned to mourning, and your joy to heaviness. Humble yourselves in the sight of the Lord, and He shall lift you up.
> (James 4:8-10)

The devil is always about his business, trying to deceive us. He's always trying to trick us into getting our focus off God. Don't be surprised at anything the devil does. His job is to wreak havoc in your life in any way possible. Just remember, your focus will either be on the things of God or the things of this world. Sacrifice yourself unto God and do not try to follow your desires.

> I beseech you therefore, brethren, by the mercies of God, that ye present your bodies a living sacrifice, holy, acceptable unto God, [which is] your reasonable service. And be not conformed to this world: but be ye transformed by the renewing of your mind, that ye may prove what [is] that good, and acceptable, and perfect, will of God.
> (Romans 12:1-2)

Set your mind on the things of the Lord, His biblical truth. Set your mind on higher things and not on the world's view. Fix your eyes on Jesus, for He is the one that has all the answers. David said:

> My eyes are fixed on you, O Sovereign Lord, in you I take refuge – do not give me over to

death. Keep me from the snares they have laid for me, from the traps set by evildoers. (Psalm 141:8-9)

The enemy will consistently try to bring havoc and confusion in our life, but we must be focused and have our minds stay on Jesus. Recognize that there is nothing new under the sun. That the adversary always has a way of laying snares in your path. He will try whatever he can to get your focus from God. The question is, will you be able to endure?

The focus will come as you learn to strive and operate in the WORD. The Whole Armor of GOD is necessary so that you will be able to stand against everything the devil tries to do and bring into your life. We need to be like the soldiers. They never think about marching into a battle without preparation. They must have their armor on them. They don't know what's before them, and they want to ensure they are covered with the necessary armor. So, it is with us spiritually. (Ephesians 6:10-18)

- The ***Helmet of Salvation***, the belief that Jesus died and rose for your sins (vs. 17)

- The ***Breastplate of Righteousness***, being honest, good, humble, and fair to others (v14)

- The ***Shield of Faith***, keep His promises without doubting Him. (v. 16)

- The ***Belt of Truth*** keeps us from the world's belief system and helps us act upon God's Word. (v. 14)

- The ***Sword of The Spirit,*** God's Word, is the offensive weapon that leads and guides us as we go forward. (v. 17)

- ***Feet Shod with The Gospel*** is our being right with God and centered in troubled times. (v. 15)

If you are not focused on God and in His will, you will not be prepared for all the distractions the adversary will bring. You need to be watchful and stay focused on what God is doing. If we were watching Him and focused on His Word and doing His Will, there are some things He would do for us:

- He will Speak to us
- He will Prepare us for HIS work.
- He will show us things that no man knows or can offer us.
- He will show us areas in our life where things are lacking.
- He will show us the good and evil within us.
- He will show us what He desires for us to do.
- He will show us whose presence we don't need to be in.
- He will show us the people that mean us no good.
- He will show us how to be strong.
- He will show us how to stay focused.

God wants us to be successful. He has a plan for us, but we need to keep our eyes focused on the vision. We must strive for and seek Him for His knowledge. The Bible shares that

> My people are destroyed for lack of knowledge. (Hosea 4:6)

We need to take the time to find out what the purpose is and what we need to do in working towards it. Anything that we lack, God has.

> If any of you lack wisdom, let him ask of God, that gives to all men liberally, and upbraids not, and it shall be given him.
> (James 1:5)

In our focus, we need to learn how to talk to God! Jesus said that He only speaks what the Father speaks. Thus, we must be willing to listen and then begin to emulate Him. As we walk by faith, we are walking according to the Word of God.

Say this prayer before you move to the next chapter!

Father, there are so many distractions around me, but I seek to keep my focus on You. Help me stay close to You so that I will not be easily distracted. When I am distracted, help me quickly get back on track as I desire to see You in Your fullness through the Bible, in Jesus' name, Amen.

Journal Your Thoughts from this Chapter Here!

_____
_____
_____
_____
_____
_____
_____
_____
_____
_____
_____

Chapter Eight

Peace I leave with you;

my peace I give unto you.

(John 14:27)

PEACE

Christ wants us to have peace of mind. When you have peace, you have freedom from quarrels and disagreements, and you are in a state of tranquility. You need to be quiet and let the Lord work. He told his disciples:

> Peace I leave with you; my peace I give unto you. (John 14:27)

Christ was tempted by Satan and frustrated by many people, but He could contain himself and show peace amid trying circumstances. People accused Him falsely and ridiculed Him, but He was able to keep

His peace. When the mob of people came and dragged Him away to kill Him, He could endure and have peace. Through it all, Jesus was able to remain peaceful and determined not to allow anyone or anything to take that peace away. Think about and respond to the below questions.

1. How many times have you allowed life circumstances to catch you off guard? Explain.

_____

_____

_____

_____

_____

2. Can you sleep when your world seems to be falling apart and the adversary breaks loose around you? Why are you able to sleep? If not, why?

_____

_____

_____

_____

_____

3. When you know there is nothing you can do about the situation, can you look to the Lord and remain peaceful in your spirit? List a few things you can do to remain peaceful.

   1. _____

   2. _____

   3. _____

Jesus said you could have the same kind of peace He had. Peace to endure, overcome, and conquer. We can have peace that surpasses all understanding if we trust in God's Word.

> For ye have need of patience, that, after ye have done the will of God, you will receive what he has promised. (Hebrews 10:36)

_____

Strengthened with all might, according to his glorious power, unto all patience and longsuffering with joyfulness;
(Colossians 1:11)

We must recognize that the concept of peace does not focus on the absence of trouble nor keep us from the trials and tribulations in life. Thus, biblical peace has nothing to do with the circumstance but with the mindset of how we look at and process it.

Paul said he could be content in any circumstance, and he demonstrated this for us when he was in jail at Philippi, where he spoke and remained confident that God was watching over him. He was able to take his focus off his situation and put it on someone else. When the opportunity arose, he shared God's goodness with the Philippian jailer and brought him and his family to salvation. James wrote that we should

Consider it all joy, my brethren, when you encounter various trials. (James 1:2)

How does one find peace during their trouble? Consider our Lord Jesus on the night before he died on the cross. He knew what He was facing, yet he still took the time to be concerned about the well-being of His disciples. Just as He was peace to them centuries ago, He still is for us. He gave them a message of peace when he said,

Peace, I leave with you; my peace I give to you; not as the world gives do I give to you. Let not your heart be troubled, neither let it be afraid. (John 14:27)

Christ also told his disciples that they would receive a Comforter when He left.

But when the Comforter comes, whom I will send unto you from the Father, even the Spirit of truth, which proceedeth from the

Father, he shall testify of me. (John 15:26)

Christ wants to bring our hearts to a place of peace in Him. This Comforter would give them peace as they endured. He told them the Holy Spirit would come to them and would be their guide through whatever they would face. They needed to be prepared, to know that they could have this peace because hard times were about to come upon them.

While conversing with one of my brothers in Christ, he shared that he had just been given an unexpected prognosis from his doctor on a routine visit. He found out that he had to have triple-bypass surgery. It could not wait. I spoke to this brother, who was sure that God had things under control. When I went to see him a couple of days after surgery, his body was weak, but his spirit was high. He remained calm and sustained peace through this physically trying time.

He is an over-comer because he trusted in the Word and believed that God would bring him through, and He did. He held on to his peace, Jesus, amid his circumstance. Peace is important because sometimes, the test can take a long time before it ends. During these times, the enemy desires to keep your mind from the things of God and wants you to focus on your current situation. Be reminded; that Satan wants to dissuade you. That is alright; it is his job. However, we must each learn to stay focused on God and let Him be our guide through every test and trial.

Say this prayer before you move to the final chapter:

Father, I need Your help and guidance to be reminded that you are the one that can keep and sustain me through the trials and tribulations of life. Even though hard times may come, help me remember to keep my mind on You so that Your peace will abound in my heart, in Jesus' name, Amen.

Journal Your Thoughts from this Chapter Here!

_____
_____
_____
_____
_____
_____
_____
_____
_____

FINAL THOUGHTS

We have made it through and are now at the end of this journey together of Victorious Living. Hopefully, you have realized that everyone goes through some struggles in life. Be mindful that even Jesus struggled as He prepared to go to the cross, and the frustrations of how a man treated Him weighed heavy on His spirit.

Negativity is all around us. These are the spiritual forces that try to bring us down. Yet, God can still bring the person through and towards their potential. When you can pull all these principles together, you will become strengthened and empowered in your thinking and actions. Thus,

Victory in Jesus is within you and surrounds your effort.

We each have the strength to endure every painful trial that comes our way as we stay in God's hands. The God of Glory will allow every problem and troubling situation that we face in this life to build us for a specific purpose. He is working out something far greater than what appears to be happening. The process of transforming you into the image of Christ is occurring.

Your faith shall be sharpened as a sword to equip you for the battles of this world. God has set the path for you. The adversary cannot destroy what God has designed for you when you are a believer and committed to Christ Jesus. Thus, as you go through, do not be anxious about anything. Look toward Him to see His mighty arms open to you, nurturing you and protecting you.

The enemy will come, but you can stand Victorious, secure because Christ died on the cross and paid for it all. Take the daily time to lift His Name in prayer with a heart of thankfulness for what He has done, is doing, and shall continue to do. He is faithful to His Word that He will never leave nor forsake you.

We can always go back to the example of the Apostle Paul. He endured and learned to wait on God to meet all his needs. He learned to be content even in suffering and persecution because he trusted Jesus Christ. There were times when he had no food or money, but He knew God was with him. He was committed to spreading the name of Jesus and was willing to ensure Christ's purpose was fulfilled.

Paul talked about the thorn that He had, and just like him, we too have thorns. Those things will not leave us, and we must endure beyond them. He is reminding us of the Glory of God in our lives and that His grace will sustain us. To have a victorious life, we must learn to put our faith in action and trust that we can make it through all things as we continue this journey in the Lord's hands.

As you end this journey on Victorious Living, take the time to write your prayer for victory based on your thoughts from what you have gleaned from these chapters!

_____

_____

_____

_____

_____

_____

_____

_____

_____

_____

_____

_____

_____

_____

_____

_____

_____

_____

_____

_____

_____

_____

_____

_____

_____

_____

Prayer for a Victorious Life

Beginning this victorious life is first based on your connections. It is about what Jesus did for you, dying on the cross. He gave His life so you can begin a victorious life in Him. He has been longing for you to become a part of His family. Jesus does not care who you are and your lifestyle; you can receive internal life. Commit your life to Him today, right this moment.

> What if though shalt confess with thy mouth the Lord Jesus. And shalt believe in thine heart that God raised him from the dead, though shalt be saved. For with the heart, man believeth unto righteousness: and confession is made unto salvation with the mouth. (Romans 10: 9-10)

Maybe you have gone through this entire book and now feel enriched. However, you have not accepted the Lord as your personal Savior. Then again, perhaps you did, but you never fully vested

yourself into His Will. If you believe that Jesus Christ died for you and are willing to give your life to Him, say the prayer below:

Lord Jesus, for too long, I've kept you out of my life. I know that I am a sinner and cannot save myself. I know that I have not been living following biblical truth. No longer will I close the door when I hear you knocking. By faith, I gratefully receive your gift of salvation. I am ready to trust you as my Lord and Savior. Thank you, Lord Jesus, for coming to earth to save my soul. I believe you are the Son of God who died on the cross for my sins and rose from the dead on the third day. Thank you for giving me the gift of eternal life. I believe your words are true. I ask You to come into my heart, Lord Jesus, and be my Savior. Amen.

I have accepted Jesus as my personal Savior on

DATE: _____

_____

I hope you keep this book and review it regularly to remind you of your commitment, prayers, and thoughts.

You have the victory, the final and complete defeat over your enemy. Thus, you know, have some fundamental principles that you can use as situations arise, be empowered for success to overcome your opponent with the Power of God!

Share your story with us at
DrAnnetteWestMinistries@gmail.com

Scripture List

Genesis 32: 24-26
Exodus 3:14
Joshua 1:1-9
Joshua 5:5
1 Samuel 17:11
1 Samuel 17:45
Job 1:6
Psalm 141:8-9
Proverbs 3:1-6
Ecclesiastes 1:9
Hosea 4:6
Matthew 3:16-17
Matthew 4:1-11
Matthew 6: 5-16
Matthew 6:33
Matthew 19:26
Luke 11:5-13
Luke 17:1
Luke 18:1-8
John 14:27
John 15:7
John 15:26
Romans 3:4
Romans 7:15-24
Romans 10: 9-10
Romans 10:17
Romans 12:1-2; 12
1 Corinthians 15:57
Galatians 5:18-21
Ephesians 6:10-18

Philippians 4:6
Colossians 1:11
I Thessalonians5:17
Hebrews 10:36
Hebrews 12:2
Hebrews 13:8
James 1:2
James 1: 12-15
James 2:17
James 4:3-10

The Lord's Prayer

Our Father which art in heaven,

Hallowed be thy name.

Thy kingdom come,

Thy will be done in earth,

as it is in heaven.

Give us this day our daily bread.

And forgive us our debts,

as we forgive our debtors.

And lead us not into temptation,

but deliver us from evil:

For thine is the kingdom,

and the power,

and the glory,

forever.

Amen

(Matthew 6:9-13)

The Visionary

Dr. Annette West

Dr. Annette is married to John, and they have three adult children. She is the CEO and Founder of JATNE Publishing, LLC., which coaches book writers, publishes books, branding and marketing, Dr. Annette had always had the heart to teach and serve others. She has a Sister's of Valor women's ministry, Marriage-Connection group, LivingWord International Outreach Ministry that supports the mission in Kakamega, Kenya, and Holistic Wellness Mind Body Spirit group.

Dr. Annette was the past radio personality with three other powerful women on Power and Praise Radio, Sumter, SC. She is the creator and voice of Living Holistically Well with Dr. West Podcast, still accessible on anchor, Apple, Spotify, and other platforms. She is the voice of The Word Fellowship every Sunday morning on Facebook, YouTube, and live streaming on Zoom.

She believes that we can "write the vision, make it plain, then run with it" because God has predestined us for greatness. (Habakkuk 2:2)

CONTACT:

Jatnepublishing.org
jatnepublishing@gmail.com
Instagram: Jatne Publishing
Face: Jatne Publishing
Clubhouse: Jatne Publishing

Other Books by Dr. Annette West

Basic Biblical Building Blocks (2002)

Centered in Christ (2020)

Centered in Christ, Devotional Steadfast ad Immovable (2021)

Entrepreneurship: Making Money God's Way in God's Time (2000)

Holistic Wellness Mind Body Spirit (2019)

Holistic Wellness Mind Body Spirit (journal) (2019)

Jesus the Path to Victorious Living (2017)

Jumpstart Your Mind (2021, coauthor)

Let the Kindompreneur Speak (2021, coauthor)

Living Words of Encouragement Vol 1 (2006)

Living Words of Encouragement Vol 2 (2016)

Marriage Connection Making it Work (2021)

23-Day Devotional The Book of Isaiah (2018)

Your Purpose Matters (2019, coauthor)

Orders books at jatnepublishing.org

Upcoming Coauthor Projects

Join our next devotional projects will be (1) Marriage Devotional and (2) Poetry book. Each publication will be written and published to help readers gain a more robust understanding of scriptures and learn ways of life application through reading stories of contributing authors and inspiration.

Joining the JATNE team of contributing authors is an opportunity for aspiring or seasoned book authors. You will be able to add your coauthored book to your shelf or another book to your marketing toolbox.

If interested, please know you will be asked to submit:

- A non-refundable but transferrable book project of a $50 fee is required to be part of the devotional project. The fee will hold your spot for the upcoming devotional publication of JATNE.
- You will be asked for professional color and a black and white headshot jpg photo.
- A brief biographical sketch of 80-100 words will need to be submitted.

We look forward to having you join the growing number of JATNE authors. Reach us at Jatnepublishing@gmail.com

Write – Writer – Writing

Maybe you've been thinking about writing a book, publishing as an individual author. If you are ready to pull thought from your mind and get it on paper, JATNE Publishing is here to assist you in getting your message out there.

We work with Christian, faith-based, inspirational writers eager to publish books with information and life application to build up the reader.

We guide you to write, publish, and launch your book in six months. You also can participate in Jumpstart Your Writing Workshop or a JATNE boot camp to learn or review the writing process.

For more information on publishing options, please email us at jatnepublishing@gmail.com

It's all about Faith – Family – Flourish to move to the next level!

www.ingramcontent.com/pod-product-compliance
Lightning Source LLC
Chambersburg PA
CBHW071021120626
46546CB00003B/1191